Jim Marshall / Jazz

Jim Marshall / Jazz

Introduction by Philip Elwood

CHRONICLE BOOKS
SAN FRANCISCO

Library of Congress Cataloging-in-Publication Data available.
0-1881-4354-8

Manufactured in Singapore.

Designed by Distinc.

Distributed in Canada by
Raincoast Books
9050 Shaughnessy Street,
Vancouver, British Columbia V6P 6E5

10 9 8 7 6 5 4 3 2 1

Chronicle Books LLC
85 Second Street,
San Francisco, California 94105
www.chroniclebooks.com

Introduction by Philip Elwood

This splendid volume of Jim Marshall's favorite jazz pictures is a nostalgic family album of the golden age of jazz, before rock-and-roll grabbed the public by the lapels and Jim cemented his fame documenting it. These photographs capture many of the jazz era's old-timers and a few of its then-newcomers—Scott LaFaro, John Handy, Michel Petrucciani, and Michael White among them—but it's not solely an elegy. Of the more than fifty performers pictured, eight are alive and still active—Vernon Alley, Handy, Jon Hendricks, Quincy Jones, Lee Konitz, Yusef Lateef, James Moody, Sonny Rollins and White—and the most famous jazz musicians never leave. Their music and personalities inspire us anew every day.

Marshall had been a dedicated jazz fan since the 1950s—his school years in San Francisco. In 1961, fresh out of a few years in the U.S. Air Force, he headed east for the first time to finally catch the jazz action in the Big Apple.

"I'd been to all the San Francisco jazz clubs like the Blackhawk, Fack's, Both/And, Jazz Workshop, all of 'em," Marshall once told me, "but I wanted to get to New York. Go to the Vanguard, the Village Gate. Get to know some of the great musicians, guys I'd never seen or heard in person."

Marshall became part of the New York jazz scene during the early '60s, but he also found that jazz was no longer the hottest musical action in town. That action had shifted to the folk music clubs and Washington Square Park in Greenwich Village. Plus, the annual Newport Jazz Festival in July was starting to get upstaged by the Newport Folk Festival a few weeks after. By 1962 and 1963 it was drawing larger, younger, and rowdier crowds than the Jazz Festivals of the '50s. To paraphrase Bob Dylan, who sang at the Newport Folk Festival in 1963, the times they were a-changin', and Jim Marshall was there.

Some of the photos in this volume come from Marshall's trip east more than forty years ago—it was to be his only extended stay (more than two years) in New York City. Even these early Marshall photos display his uncanny ability to capture the mood, personality, and soul of an artist, in much the same way that a few brilliant music producers have developed the knack of getting the very best from an artist in the blandness of a recording studio.

It's not a coincidence that most of the pictures in this album were taken in recording studios, rehearsal halls, backstage areas, festival grounds, or home living rooms; noticeably fewer are onstage performances.

Marshall often admits his lifelong enthusiasm for not just getting a "how'r ya" from a performer but, rather, becoming a backstage friend—hanging out with musicians, getting to know them and their colleagues, and often, developing a friendship with their families.

His photos radiate with this informal, friendly intimacy—they are like family snapshots, and in at least one case, expressly so.

To know Jim Marshall and observe him at work, Leica M4 in hand, paraphernalia nearby or dangling from his shoulder, can be both fascinating, unnerving, and occasionally entertaining in itself.

More than once at various venues I have seen ushers, burly guards, stage managers, and concert impresarios—all with (perhaps) an even shorter fuse than the tempestuous Marshall—attempt to remove Jim from the stage. Of course, these efforts are most often unsuccesful; Jim never just stands by the stage lip waiting for shots to appear.

Since its inception, the Monterey Jazz Festival has provided excellent onstage and stage-lip photo ops for working photographers; Marshall, in fact, was the event's official photographer in the years bracketing his New York stay, and many of this collection's shots, on- and offstage, were taken at Monterey.

But Marshall's idea of capturing action on any stage, whether at Monterey or Manhattan's Avery Fisher Hall, does not involve poking his lens through an eight-inch hole in a bandshell or hovering around in a crowded photo pit, waiting his turn.

Only he would crawl through the Duke Ellington brass section while they're playing to get a facial shot of the Duke at the keyboard, snapped under the lid from the tip of the grand piano, strings in the foreground.

And, who else but Jim Marshall would conceive a picture that captured the head-and-shoulders of Ray Charles at the keyboard, spotlight-silhouetted on the bass drumhead at the rear of the band?

And then, there is the 1966 shot of Gil Evans at the piano in a desolate, barny exhibit hall on the Monterey County Fairgrounds, working over arrangements while awaiting his bandsmen for the night's concert so they could rehearse.

Here, we do not see this giant of jazz as a big-band pianist on Monterey's Arena stage in front of eight thousand fans; rather, Marshall captures Evans at work in the role that made him one of the masters of modern jazz: that of composer-arranger.

Monterey Jazz regulars learned early on that some of the festival's most fascinating experiences were the rehearsal sessions in one or another of the County Fairgrounds' exhibit halls. One year, after they saw a couple of Marshall's photos and my review of a particularly chaotic Charles Mingus rehearsal, they jammed the hall, leading authorities to declare rehearsals off-limits. Marshall, naturally, continued to photograph them.

In the same way that Marshall's shot of Evans is precisely the right setting for the famous composer-arranger, his onstage shot of tenor saxophonist Paul Gonsalves with his bandleader Duke Ellington (at the 1960 Monterey Jazz Festival) is likewise perfect.

Seeing this photo, a viewer wonders: Why is the radiant Duke shouting and clapping as Gonsalves is blowing up a sweat? Why is Ellington acting as a yell leader, indicating numbers with his fingers? Marshall, with this one picture, generates curiosity and enthusiasm at the same time.

My take—Gonsalves must be playing his jazz-world famous twenty-seven tenor sax solo choruses on the Duke's vintage chart, "Diminuendo and Crescendo in Blue," which had highlighted the 1956 Newport Festival.

That few minutes of saxophone soloing at Newport made Gonsalves an Ellington star for years to come. It was this performance at Newport that revived public enthusiasm for all of Duke Ellington's music as well as his "Famous Orchestra" itself. These were times when the few remaining big bands were fading away, like old soldiers.

"I was born at the Newport Jazz Festival on July 7th, 1956," wrote Ellington after publicity of the sensational event spread around the jazz world.

Marshall's picture of the sweating Gonsalves wailing out his solo with Duke acting as the event's yell leader tells the whole story in a single frame.

Marshall's love of hanging out with jazz musicians provided him with opportunities to photograph them not only informally, out of the spotlight, but also to receive their blessing to shoot them at will in performance, spending a whole set or two (and many rolls of film) in the effort to capture what he felt was that one definitive image.

Look, for instance, at the glowing, guffawing faces of trumpeter Cootie Williams, pianist Count Basie, and singer Billy Eckstine—they've just heard a rich, perhaps ribald, backstage joke and Jim's camera-eye seems to be laughing along with them. Another good-time shot is that of Monk, Gillespie, and Gerald Wilson—and note the core (Congress of Racial Equality) "Freedom Now" badge on Diz's lapel, a reminder of times long gone.

In the shot of Jon Hendricks and Hollywood comic-actress Martha Raye, Marshall not only captured a great pair of singers, but a couple who appeared together so infrequently that they were never photographed elsewhere.

In his usual radiant mood, Basie's fine singer "Mr. Five-by-Five," Jimmy Rushing, is captured by Marshall leading a late-night crowd in a sing-and-clap-along; and there's also the particular joyousness in the on-stage shot of Roberta Flack and Donny Hathaway, Marshall's camera catching not just the fun but also the mutual admiration this pair had for each other.

And, who can help but snicker at the joy that is communicated by Carmen McRae and Dizzy Gillespie in the basement dressing room of San Francisco's Great American Music Hall? Check out Diz's outrageous attire (how 'bout those threads!) and pose—in one hand a cigar, in the other both of Carmen's hands.

Marshall's close relationships with the jazz crowd got him pictures the likes of which no one else could have taken.

Of many great John Coltrane portraits that Marshall has taken (and that have been used for LP covers issued by a dozen labels), one of my favorites shows 'Trane in thought, finger on his lip, eyes looking ahead, thoughts maybe somewhere far from Ralph Gleason's living room in Berkeley—or is Coltrane absorbed in the ongoing conversation?

Either way, Marshall has a knack for capturing reflective moods. Another classic is of the great tenor saxophonist Coleman Hawkins as he sits in a barren dressing room, smoking under the No Smoking sign. Hawkins died in 1969, a few years after the photo was taken, burned out. He'd been playing professionally since he was twelve years old, since 1916; he first recorded in 1922 with Mamie Smith's Jazz Hounds—and through Marshall's lens, we can see the toll of every one of those fifty years living the jazz life.

Similarly, study the photo of a forlorn Sammy Davis Jr. in his dressing room, bedecked with rings and chains, surrounded by mirrors, his blank, emotionless, staring eyes gazing nowhere. "There's no business like show business, is there, Mr. Bojangles?"

There are five photos of Thelonious Monk in this collection: First, a classic shot with Allen Ginsberg in which both seem mesmerized by the other's presence. Then there's the picture of Monk, Dizzy Gillespie, and Philly Joe Jones—a good-time shot of old friends—which is followed by Monk pacing a recording studio, either listening to a playback (unlikely) or just thinking.

Monk at the keyboard is next, with Marshall's focus on Monk's hand, his immense MONK ring on one finger, a cigarette held by two more fingers; he is, of course, playing the piano at the same time.

The last Monk shot is of his whole family—but the focus, really, is on Monk's pride in his wife and children. Jim Marshall catches that pride on Monk's face beautifully.

Recalling the star-jammed 1963 Monterey Jazz Festival—which presented the MJQ; Lambert, Hendricks, and Bavan; Gerald Wilson's Orchestra; Gerry Mulligan Quartet; Monk's Quartet; Carmen McRae, Dizzy Gillespie, Dave Brubeck and others (!), all of whom Marshall photographed—Jim once commented, "One of the most emotional photos I've ever taken was that year at Monterey when Jack Teagarden, his mother Helen, sister Norma, and brother Charlie gathered together for a picture."

Jack and Charlie were part of the weekend program, and Helen and Norma came down for a family get-together.

"What a sweetheart Norma was," Marshall continued. "She was worried about Jack's failing health and wanted a family picture taken."

Years later I asked Norma (who was the personification of what Jim identified as "a real sweetheart") about the Monterey picture. She recalled that she had wanted a "more formal family picture, something we never had." But in the end, after the shots had been printed up, her favorite was the quite informal one that showed the four Teagardens laughing and chatting, family-style.

Jack died just a few months after the 1963 Monterey Festival. Helen and Charlie lived into the early 1980s, and Norma (who lived her last twenty years in San Francisco) was still playing piano into the 1990s. She died at eighty-five in 1995.

Marshall still gets tearful recalling that cloudy Monterey afternoon forty years ago. So do I—John Hammond and I were together, watching the shot being taken. Hammond had recorded Jack more than thirty years earlier and was still a big fan of Big T, but we both wondered how long Jack's health would hold.

Marshall captured those years, that mood, that resignation, with a few clicks of the shutter.

In this volume, Jim Marshall has not only given us an invaluable photo album; he has also enabled those thousands of jazz lovers on the outside a glimpse inside a long-passed world of jazz.

"Here's one of my favorite pictures. John Coltrane, taken at the home of Ralph Gleason, the late *Chronicle* jazz critic in 1960. John and I had met at the Jazz Workshop and we were talking backstage. John says, 'Well, I gotta do an interview with Ralph Gleason tomorrow, how do I get to Berkeley?' I said, 'I'll drive you.' So I picked him up at the hotel and drove him, and that's where I took the pictures."

Anita O'Day,
San Francisco, 1960.

15.

Annie Ross at the Jazz Workshop,
San Francisco, 1960.

Johnny Hodges at the
Monterey Jazz Festival, 1960.

John Coltrane
at Ralph Gleason's house,
Berkeley, 1960.

Blue Mitchell
at the Blackhawk,
San Francisco, 1960.

Bass player Paul Chambers at the Jazz Workshop, San Francisco, n.d.

Bev Kelly and Pony Poindexter
at the Coffee Gallery, San Francisco, n.d.

Al Gray at
Russ Wilson's house,
San Francisco, 1961.

Right: Helen Humes at the
Jazz Workshop, San Francisco,
1959 or 1960.

Red Norvo,
San Francisco, 1959 or 1960.

"Here, Zoot Sims stops by to say hello to Stan Getz during a 1963 photo shoot. These two great tenor players, the two best white tenor players, were both former members of Woody Herman's Four Brothers."

Rahsaan Roland Kirk and Pearl Bailey
at the Las Vegas Jazz Festival, 1962.

Dinah Washington
at the Masonic Auditorium,
San Francisco, 1959.

"I shot John Coltrane at Rudy Van Gelder's studio in New York, during an ABC Records' session for Impulse! in 1963. He's listening to the playback of 'Nancy with the Laughing Face.'"

"Here, one of the most important piano players, Red Garland, plays with the Red Garland Trio at the Jazz Workshop in San Francisco, 1959. The waitress at the Jazz Workshop used to put a red rose in a vase every day on the piano."

Scott LaFaro at the
Monterey Jazz Festival, 1960.

"Here Ray Charles is just a silhouette on the drums. This was a one-grab shot in New York City around 1962."

Jimmy Witherspoon at the
Monterey Jazz Festival, 1960.

Horace Silver
at Russ Wilson's house,
San Francisco, 1960.

Mel Torme,
Las Vegas, 1961 or 1962.

Yusef Lateef, Cannonball Adderley, and Nat Adderley backstage at the Las Vegas Jazz Festival, n.d.

Jim Hall
at a Mingus recording session, n.d.

Right: Steve Lacy in
his apartment in New York City, 1963.

"This is Coleman Hawkins backstage at the Village Gate in New York City, 1963. There were five or six clubs within five or six blocks of each other and I used to go from one to the other to just hang out and go backstage and take pictures. No one said anything. Evidently, Coleman had quite a reputation, but he was always nice to me."

Louis Armstrong backstage at the
Monterey Jazz Festival, 1966.

King Pleasure and Jon Hendricks,
New York City, 1963.

"Here's another obscure musician named Pete Brown. There was a benefit for a musician on Sunday afternoon in 1963 and Dizzy was onstage, saw Mr. Brown come in with his horn in a bag, stopped the show, and brought Pete up on the stage with him and blew the place away. He was as good as Charlie Parker, but Dizzy was the only one that recognized him. That's what's amazing about Gillespie. He had such a reverence for the older guys, you know, just amazing."

"Here's Ben Webster at the Five Spot on 8th Street in New York City. This is one of my favorite shots, taken at a Sunday afternoon jam session in 1963."

Left: Charles Lloyd
in his apartment,
New York City, 1964.

Percy Heath
at the Coffee Gallery,
San Francisco, 1960.

Hank Crawford backstage with a fan
at the Oakland Coliseum, 1960.

"Here's Miles Davis talking shit, probably about some chick, to Steve McQueen backstage at the Monterey Jazz Festival, 1963."

Elmo Hope
at the Village Gate,
New York City, 1963.

52.

Left: Ray Charles backstage at the Longshoremen's Hall, San Francisco, 1961.

Oscar Peterson backstage at the Las Vegas Jazz Festival, 1962.

Hank Crawford at a
Ray Charles recording session,
New York City, 1962.

"This is Ray Charles backstage, 1962.
I think it was in Long Island."

Count Basie at the
Longshoremen's Hall,
San Francisco, 1966.

Monk, Dizzy Gillespie, and Gerald Wilson backstage at the Monterey Jazz Festival, 1963.

Jimmy Rushing at the
Monterey Jazz Festival, 1960.

Chico Hamilton
at a Rudy Van Gelder's studio
recording session for Impulse!,
New York City, 1963.

Al Cohn behind a club,
New York City, 1963.

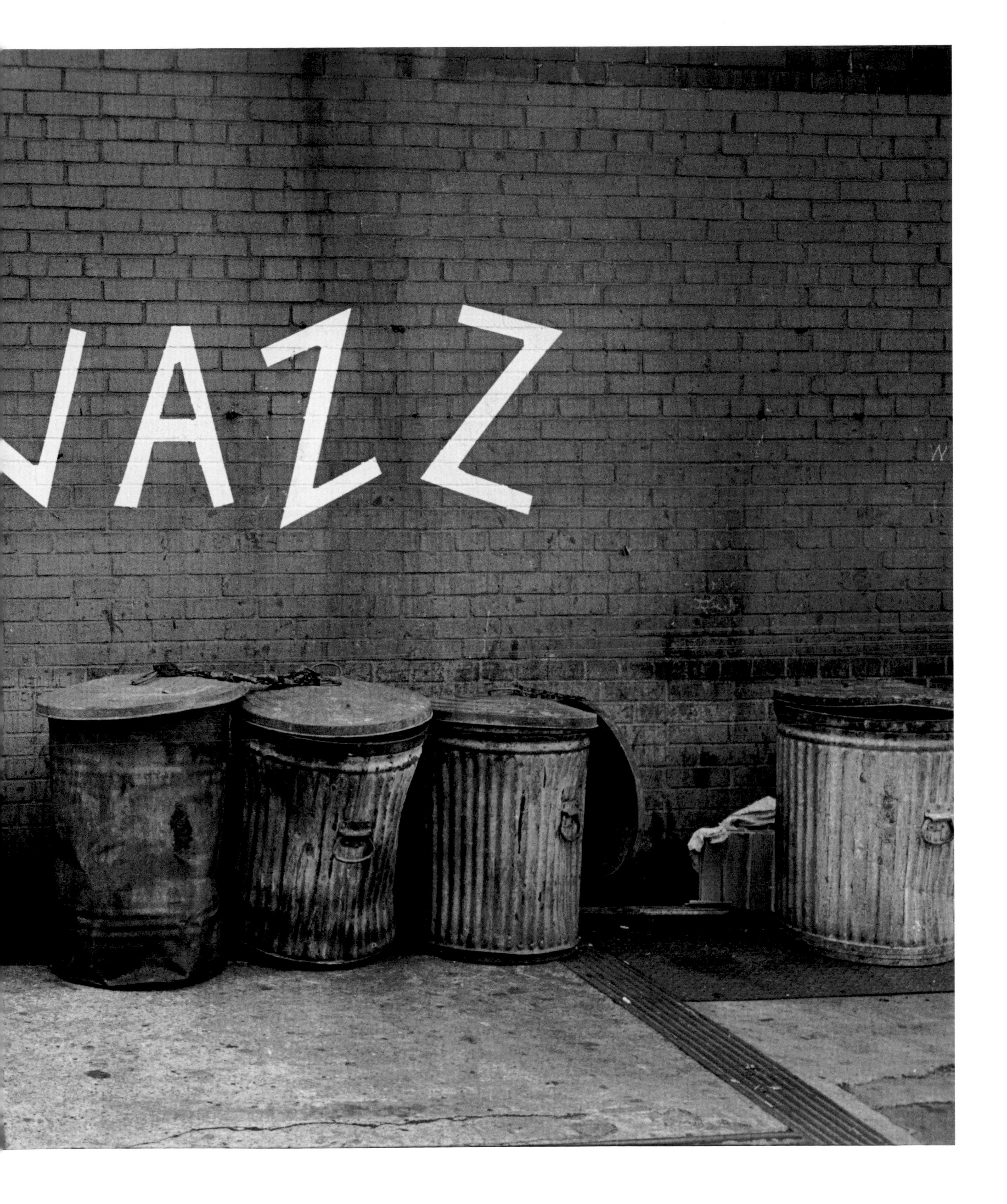
JAZZ

"Here's Miles Davis having his cigarette lit by Harry James. This was backstage at the Monterey Jazz Festival in 1963. They're just below an overhead light and I shot it with a quarter-second exposure."

Right:
Eric Dolphy backstage at the Village Gate, New York City, 1962.

63.

Miles Davis in his
New York City apartment, 1963.

Ray Brown,
New York City, 1962.

Bill Evans at a
Riverside Records recording session,
New York City, 1963.

"This is arranger and composer Gil Evans at the Monterey Jazz Festival in 1966. Evans was warming up in a large rehearsal hall backstage."

"I shot Jack Teagarden, his mother, Mama T, his sister, Norma, and his brother, Charlie, backstage at the Monterey Jazz Festival in 1963. Jack died shortly after this picture was taken in the early part of '64, about six months later. There was a recording called 'A Hundred Years From Today.' It was a song that Teagarden had had a big hit with during World War II. There's a line, 'Don't save your kisses, just give them away,' and then there's another line, 'Who'll ever know you gave them away a hundred years from today?' He tells the story at the jazz festival about how, during the war, a soldier in England came up to him and requested that song."

“Originally photographed for a *Saturday Evening Post* feature in 1963, Monk sits at his piano dressed in a silk robe. The piano was kept in the kitchen of his small, three-bedroom apartment in New York City.”

"Here's Monk kinda just wistfully waltzing around the studio. Columbia recorded Monk at an old church on 30th Street in New York City that had been desanctified or something. The pictures from that session, including this one of Monk listening to playback, were taken in late 1962 or 1963 and were then misfiled at Columbia Records. They had been lost for forty years until they found them last year."

"This is Thelonious Monk, his daughter, wife, and son in the kitchen of his apartment on 60th Street in New York City. This was in 1963 for a *Saturday Evening Post* feature, originally. Monk was impenetrable for me. I don't think I ever had fifty words with him. But he was very accessible to me, evidently, because I think that some of these old jazz guys realized that I just wanted to make good pictures. There was no restriction, and I think that was pretty important. There wasn't a lot of bullshit to go through, and I think they trusted me. Obviously."

Monk at the Columbia Records'
recording studio, New York, 1963.

Monk at the
Monterey Jazz Festival, 1964.

"This is Monk's hand on the piano keys, taken in his apartment on 60th Street in 1963. Notice how the diamonds in his ring spell out 'MONK'."

Jim Hall and Paul Desmond
at the RCA Recording Studios,
New York City, 1962 or 1963.

David "Fathead" Newman at a
Ray Charles recording session, 1963.

"I shot Duke Ellington and Paul Gonsalves at the Monterey Jazz Festival in 1960. Paul played almost his whole career with Duke; this was taken during one of Paul's extended solos."

Elvin Jones at the
Monterey Jazz Festival, 1966.

"This is Miriam Makeba at the Monterey Jazz Festival in 1960, singing 'Evolution of the Blues.' She had just come from South Africa, an Xhosa tribe woman."

Jimmy Witherspoon at the
Monterey Jazz Festival, 1964.

"This was taken backstage at the Monterey Jazz Festival in 1963. Allen Ginsberg is looking at Thelonious Monk like he's looking at God. There are two frames. I walked by him and took bang! bang! two shots, that's it. But it's like he's looking at God."

Left: Dave Brubeck backstage at the Newport Jazz Festival, 1963.

Duke Ellington at the Monterey Jazz Festival, 1966.

Coltrane at the
Balance recording session
in Van Gelder's studio,
New Jersey, 1963.

Stan Kenton at a rehearsal
at the Monterey Jazz Festival, 1964.

87.

Michael White and John Handy in a shot used on Handy's *Live at the Monterey Jazz Festival* album, Monterey Jazz Festival, 1965.

McCoy Tyner at the
Newport Jazz Festival, 1963.

Duke Ellington at the Monterey Jazz Festival, 1966.

Chuck Isreal at the Village Gate,
New York City, 1963.

Right: Bill Evans at a
RCA recording session,
New York City, 1961.

Joe Williams,
San Francisco, 1961 or 1962.

Miles Davis
at Newman's Gym on Leavenworth
Street in San Francisco, 1970.

"Here, Miles is in the ring at Newman's Gym in San Francisco in 1971. Doesn't exist anymore. It was like a sister to a famous gym in New York where pros went that was called Stillman's. At Newman's Gym, Miles used to work out. He used to box with guys, 'Don't hit me in the mouth, I gotta play tonight.'"

Miles at
Winterland, San Francisco, 1971.

Miles backstage at the
Berkeley Community Theater, 1971.

Miles at Newman's Gym,
San Francisco, 1971.

Eric Dolphy at a
Mingus Town Hall performance
rehearsal, New York, 1963.

Melba Liston at a
Mingus recording session, 1962.

James Moody at a
Mingus recording session,
New York City, 1963.

Louie Bellson at the
Monterey Jazz Festival, 1966.

"I took this shot of John Coltrane backstage at Stanford University in early 1966, a few months before he died."

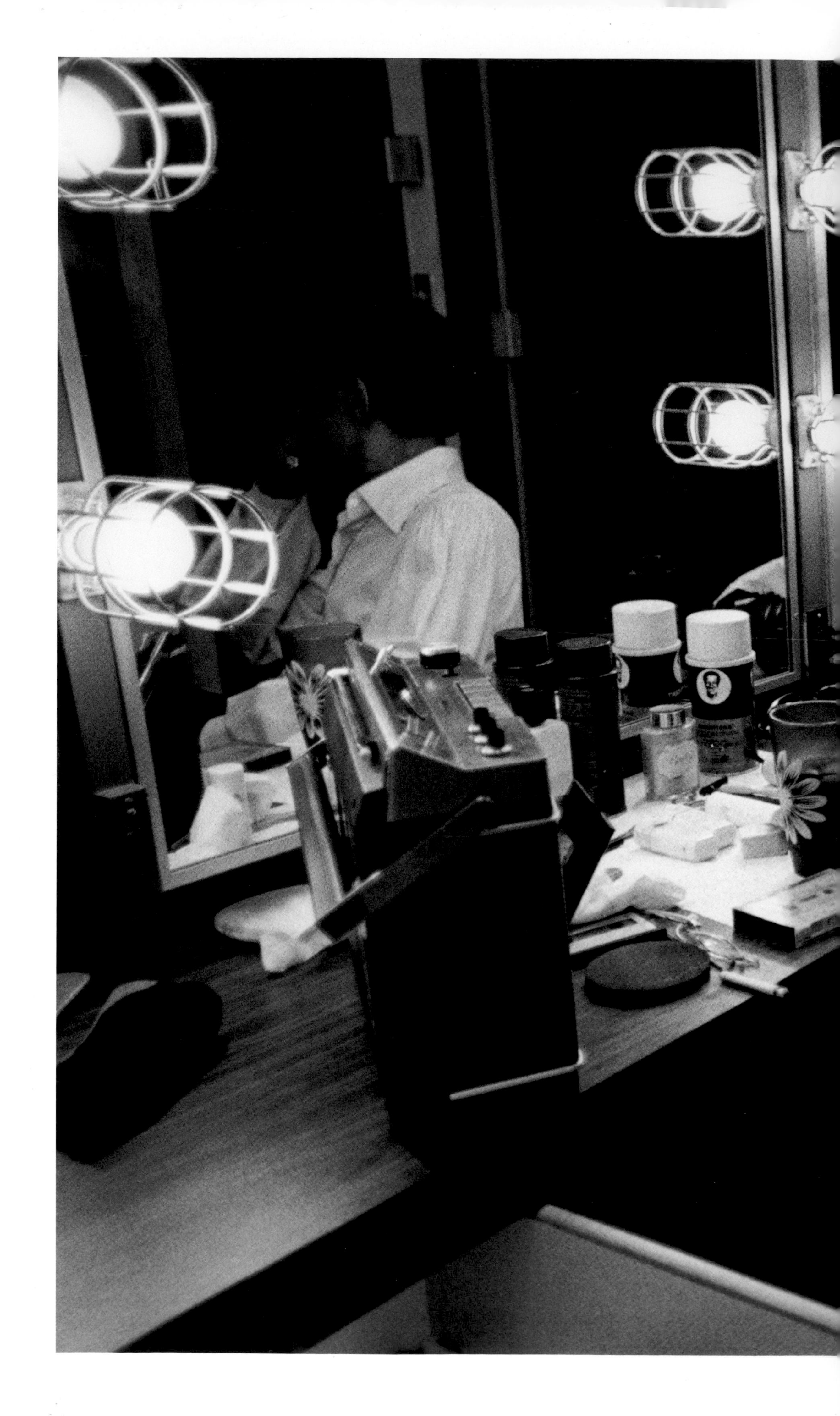

Sammy Davis Jr. backstage
at the Duke Ellington tribute at
CBS TV Studios, Los Angeles, 1972.

Mingus at the
UC Jazz Festival at the Greek Theater,
Berkeley, 1966.

"This is Jon Hendricks and Martha Raye at Trident in Sausalito, California, recording a live album for Mercury Records in 1965. Jon said, 'Ladies and gentlemen, I want to bring up a guest artist to sing with me. Ladies and gentlemen, Miss Martha Raye.' People kinda snickered. Man, she blew the place away. I mean, I was just stunned. I'd never heard her."

Lee Konitz
at a club in Monterey, 1966.

Joe Newman
at the Five Spot, New York City, 1963.

Jackie McLean at the
Monterey Jazz Festival, 1966.

“Here are Roberta Flack and Donny Hathaway in 1972. I think it might’ve been Berkeley, but I don’t remember.”

Left: Monk backstage at the Monterey Jazz Festival, 1966.

Paul Gonsalves backstage at the Duke Ellington tribute at CBS TV Studios, Los Angeles, 1972.

Quincy Jones and Peggy Lipton
backstage at the Duke Ellington
tribute at CBS TV Studios,
Los Angeles, 1972.

Count Basie and Paul Gonsalves backstage at the Duke Ellington tribute at CBS TV Studios, Los Angeles, 1972.

John Handy
at his Baker Street home,
San Francisco, 1967.

"This is King Curtis at an Aretha Franklin recording session in New York or Los Angeles. He was a very ebullient guy; it was just amazing. He was killed, stabbed to death in his doorway, when he tried to break up a fight between two Puerto Rican guys."

121.

Cootie Williams, Count Basie, and Billy Eckstine, backstage at the Duke Ellington tribute, CBS TV Studios, Los Angeles, 1972.

"This is Marcus Belgrave, who worked with Ray Charles off and on for decades, in New York in 1962."

Mingus at the
Monterey Jazz Festival, 1964.

Vernon Alley
at Steve Hathaway's studio in
San Francisco, late 1990s.

Sonny Payne at the
Longshoremen's Hall,
San Francisco, 1960.

Jon Hendricks at the
Monterey Jazz Festival, 1966.

Sonny Rollins at the
Great American Music Hall,
San Francisco, early 1980s.

Teddy Edwards at the
Monterey Jazz Festival, 1964.

Stanley Turrentine at the
Great American Music Hall,
San Francisco, early 1980s.

"In 1976, Carmen McRae was performing at the Great American Music Hall in San Francisco; the show was being recorded for a live album. Dizzy Gillespie was a guest artist. This was in the dressing room, in the basement."

Gabor Zabo,
San Francisco, 1965 or 1966.

"I shot Michel Petrucciani at Ken Schubert's house in the late 1980s. Michel was a French dwarf and an incredible piano player. He accessed the pedals by placing blocks on them."

Illinois Jacquet and John Lewis
of the Modern Jazz Quartet at the
Monterey Jazz Festival, 1966.

Sonny Rollins and Donald Byrd
at the Great American Music Hall,
San Francisco, early 1980s.

"This is Woody Herman at the Monterey Jazz Festival in 1966 or 1967. I love his energy. He always had great swing bands with incredible musicians in them, like Stan Kenton and Billy Eckstine."

Frank Morgan at the
UC Jazz Festival, Berkeley, 1980s.

Sarah Vaughan at the
Cow Palace, San Francisco,
late 1980s.

Arthur Prysock through the window of a coffee shop for one of his mid-1980s releases on Milestone.

Right: Monk at West 30th Street, New York City, 1963.

141.

Acknowledgments

I lived in New York from June of 1962 to December 1964. It was a great time—going to two or three clubs a night with no restrictions on taking photos. It was a time we will not see again. Nor will we see these kinds of photos. Some of these photos are from the first rolls I ever shot—the Dinah Washington is from Roll 40. The music was my passion—the camera my instrument.

I've said it before and I'll say it again—I'm not a rock photographer. I usually follow that up with a joke about how Ansel Adams is a rock photographer—maybe you've heard that one.

This book may come as a surprise to those who think they know all about my work. Sure, I have pictures of jazz artists that are well-known, especially of Miles, Coltrane, and Monk, but here are a lot that most people have never seen. I want these jazz photos to be thought of as a significant part of my career. I put a lot into them. In turn, I've tried to capture the intensity and elegance of these people.

I thank the following people for helping make this book possible:

Phil Elwood for his words and expert memory
Kirk Anspach for his excellent printing
Amelia Davis
Bob Thiele
Orrin Keepnews
John Berg and Bob Cato of Columbia Records
Bert Block
Nion McEvoy and Alan Rapp at Chronicle Books